Good morni

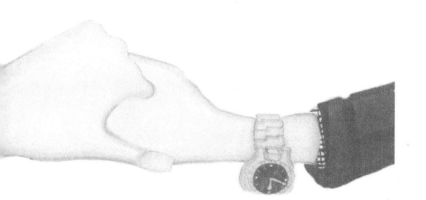

Eleni Sophia Kaur

There was something about holding his hand that made her feel as if she was at home

Good morning to Goodnight- Eleni Kaur

I write because words are my lifeline, they're my catharsis and my therapy. Without them, I would have no voice and no outlet to express my soul. The gratification and the getaway from the authentic world is so unique; one can simply create their own utopian culture, whilst escaping a dystopian society. Writing is a great form of communiqué. It is an incredible sort of escapism and therefore one of the best forms of liberty. I write because occasionally I have things worth saying but writing is what prompts me to express them. There is a narcissistic pleasure of writing and I personally write to help make the world a better place. There are no restrictions and I have the ability to express the lessons I have learned, the adversity and hardships I have witnessed people endure and I don't want my individual understandings to go to waste.

That is why I write.

Good morning to Goodnight- Eleni Kaur

I find it absolutely astonishing that good morning consists of two words whereas goodnight is composed of only one.

When thinking about this significant other being my 'good morning' to 'goodnight,' I looked deeper into it and admired the metaphorical ambiguity it presented when compared to our relationship.

The morning is a blessing- it's how I felt whilst in the relationship; I looked forward to waking up and starting a new day- I looked forward to a 'good morning.' The night was when we opened up and let one another in. We told each other our deepest longings and our biggest fears- which united us.

After the night there is always hope for a morning. So, even if this separation is a long, dark nightmare, maybe in a few years' time, he and I will find our morning.

Or, maybe I just have to come to terms with the idea that we weren't written to be for this world.

Good morning to Goodnight- Eleni Kaur

I don't know.

Good morning to Goodnight- Eleni Kaur

I didn't want the memories we created to float around my mind- a place they would gradually fade. So, I decided to write this- I took inspiration from what we had and crafted them into this book.

Despite my poems having many simplistic elements, I have been told that my words 'speak for themselves.' The poetry itself was driven by strong emotions and I really hope my writing is relatable.

Although it is easy for readers to automatically assume what writers are articulating is something they've personally been through, isn't necessarily true. Our enthusiasm is driven from what we see around us as, as well as our own experiences.

You've probably realized this collection was of course inspired by a particular event in my life as well as a certain individual. But, I would like to clarify that I have a lot of respect for him and I would never intentionally do anything to disrespect him in any way- I presume you could say I wrote this to prove a point- I don't give up easily and if I want something, I'll fight for it and I really hope I demonstrate that throughout the book. I guess you could also say this is my final attempt before I completely take my step back. This way, at least I can say that I tried.

I would, however, like to point out that not every poem in here is about us. Yes, inspiration was taken from what we had but I have tried to write in such a way that many of you around the world can relate.

Therefore, I hope that by the end of the book you can take something from my writing. I have tried to express myself in such a way that I can inspire other individuals to never give up on what they truly love and believe in. I hope you realize that you can still remain strong- no matter how far down you may fall.

I love sharing my writing and hoping other personalities around the world can relate; I feel as if it almost brings us together- it makes us strong.

I don't see myself as frail by writing this. Although some poems were written at my weakest of times, I believe composing all these feelings is an act of strength rather than one of weakness.

I want you to take a look at yourself; take a moment to reflect on how far you have come. You may have loved, you may have been broken and you are now on the journey to finding yourself.

Good morning to Goodnight- Eleni Kaur

A saying I have repeated within this book is 'everything happens for a reason and whatever is meant to be, will be.' Maybe whoever or whatever came to mind when reading what I previously wrote will come back. Maybe this departure was necessary for you both to find yourselves and then come find one another. Or, maybe it just wasn't meant to be. As difficult as this may be to comprehend, one day someone will come along and show you why it never worked out with another; one day it will all make sense.

Nevertheless, I promise you, no matter how difficult your situation may be, you will progress; 'there is always light at the end of a tunnel.'

I hope you enjoy my collection

Lots of love,

Eleni
x

First Love

Your first love is an individual to
whom you wholly open up to-
Not only in the sense that you tell
them about certain things in your life
But,
They see everything.
They're the first to witness it too-
The way you love.
They're the first to witness how
you love!
It won't be the same with anyone
else. No matter how hard you try to
tell yourself that it will- it will never be
the same
You don't love the same as you did
your first.
Predominantly because you learn
things over time that changes your
approach towards this very crazy thing
called Love.
But
They got to see the innocent
side, The pure side,
They were fortunate enough to see
what you believed love would be like

Good morning to Goodnight- Eleni Kaur

and if you're lucky enough
They won't forget you
They won't forget the love you
gave them

For The Boy in the Blue Suit From The Girl in the Maroon Scarf

This one's dedicated to the man who
I met not so long ago.

The one who made me feel as if I
had known him for years.

The man who I valued with all my
heart-my first.

The man I was prepared to look
after and take care of for eternity.

This one's for the man who gently made me
fall in love with my insecurities.

This one's for the man I fell in love with
entirely, utterly, exclusively

This is for the man who it all comes
down to

This one's for you.

Building You

I want to help you grow as an individual;
every single part of you means
everything to me.
I want to help you grow mentally and
spiritually.
I want to be the girl who has your back
during your struggles and motivates you
to keep going.
I want to help you become a better
individual- I want to help strengthen
your belief, your knowledge.
I want to build you.
I want to build you in terms of faith and
therefore the connection between
yourself and God.
I want God to look after you- I want him
to be there for you when you're at your
lowest of lows and highest of highs!
But, I also want you to remember him
daily.
I want you to thank him for everything
you have and make it a habit- for he
will be the one to guide you in the right
path.

Good morning to Goodnight- Eleni Kaur

Unexpected calls-

Looking out the window

Knees on ground

Biggest smile

Gazing up towards the sky

One hand on phone

The other resting upon the
warm radiator

It's the unexpected moments like this
that she doesn't want to end

The effortless moments
she cherishes

A simple phone call or notification
from you makes her feel like the
happiest girl alive

Holding her hand and kissing her
forehead
She loved it when you did
that Hands held so tight
Smile facing the ground
Your lips on her forehead
Gentlemanlike.
She loved it.
Protected.
Secure.
When it was just you and her.

Good morning to Goodnight- Eleni Kaur

Waves of pleasure
Goosebumps all over
Shivering body
Delight
Slow moans
Deep breathing
Only desired to be experienced with
one individual

The way he bit her lip and wrapped
his lips right around hers- saliva all
over Her heart had never beaten
faster She breathed heavily and
enjoyed every moment

Good morning to Goodnight- Eleni Kaur

Oh when he laid his hands upon her
biggest insecurity telling her he loved it

The insecurity she hated due to
society's expectations of a 'woman'

The way he squeezed it and held it
in his hands with such love

This is sexy he said

She'll never forget that moment

Reassuring her there was nothing for
her to feel so unconfident about

Good morning to Goodnight- Eleni Kaur

Oh when he laid his hands upon my
biggest insecurity and told me he
'loved it'

I felt as if I were at home

I had never felt so loved

Good morning to Goodnight- Eleni Kaur

The way you felt so happy and warm
At the thought of loving someone.
They're the one person who you're
going to love wholeheartedly- the
person to whom you give such a piece
of your heart to that it'll forever
remain. If you're one of the lucky
ones, they'll never forget you
They won't forget how you loved them.

Good morning to Goodnight- Eleni Kaur

When my hand first touched

yours Soft.

I write this with the picture in front
of me.

Hands entwined

Your thumb, resting on my

fingers My thumb,

laying at the back of your hands

It lasted seconds

But felt like no other feeling

I felt as though I was

secure.

Forever and Ever.

Good morning to Goodnight- Eleni Kaur

She sought nothing but of his

companionship

She didn't wish for anything but his time

She desired his presence

She embraced him

She loved him

O how very deep her love was- love of
a 'crazy girl' they all said-

'We've never seen someone love this
much'

They continued

Good morning to Goodnight- Eleni Kaur

She didn't want to be touched by
another;
Nobody else's presence excited her
as even the thought of yours did
She didn't want anybody else's
lips on hers
The idea of somebody else's
touch tightened and clenched her
throat (She was afraid.)
She was so in love with your embrace
She didn't want anyone else to rub
her back whilst they hugged
Let alone be in anyone else's arms

She wanted you
Only you

Good morning to Goodnight- Eleni Kaur

His delicate warm touch upon the flower
stroking slowly yet with intensified pace:
petals start blowing- as if being moved
by the winds
Slowly yet passionately
waves of pleasure
O how the flower loved it
Before the flower even knew what the
hand felt like, the pollen was pre-
burst He continued caressing
As the pollen continued
to leak
Faster pace
He added more fingers to
continue rubbing
Anther stigma filament petal
all aroused
Just from one delicate touch
from one delicate individual to a flower
that urged to be valued for its
presence and all that it could offer
three or four fingers- stroking
From the individual to-the flower whose
love came right from the roots

Good morning to Goodnight- Eleni Kaur

The way my hands ran lusciously
through your hair

The way you didn't like anyone touching
your hair

But I still did it.

'You like it really'

'It feels like a head

massage' Soft hair

Dark brown eyes

A perfect picture I'll forever remember

O how can one human have such an effect?

I remember the way he called me beautiful and told me that I'll go far in life. I was touched- touched on a different level- more than a physical touch- It was as if these words heartened my soul. Words, a voice, his emotional touch, his essence

I'll never forget

Her Mindset

I think many men forget that a woman's mindset will bring up their children. It's their mentality that will teach them how to raise their children with the courtesy of being polite, respectful.

Yes, beauty is a bonus. But, external beauty fades.

It's the mindset that'll not only benefit them by inspiring them, keeping them on the right path and lending them an arm when they need a hand but will raise the mini-them.

That's what they forget.

Her mindset

Mindset before beauty.

External beauty will fade
Internal beauty will forever remain.

Choose sensibly.

Good morning to Goodnight- Eleni Kaur

A man's success is reflected from the woman he chooses to have by his side. I hope to God whoever you choose brings out the best in you. I hope she loves you unconditionally.

Because I was brought up to recognize the best in people

To wish people the very best

No matter how much pain your departure may have caused

My love for you is incessant

You never notice how fragile you are
until you hear something you thought
you'd never have to and lose
something you were terrified of losing

Good morning to Goodnight- Eleni Kaur

She dreamed he lay her gently in bed
Deeply gazing into her eyes
Above her
Moving her hair gently from her face
to behind her ear
Bringing himself closer
His breathing reflecting his warmth onto
her gentle sensitive skin
Eyes closed
Lips pressing against one
another's Slow motion,
He picks himself up slightly
Holds her hands above her
head Slow,
Gentle
One another's embrace
Hands held tight above her
head He takes control
He protects.
He's in charge
She liked that.
One hand around throat
The other above her head
(She enjoyed that)
Moans
Pleasure
Embraced and Entwined
Enduringly

It was an act neither of them wanted to do- it wasn't as simple as them both loving one another and everything being perfect- it was far more complicated

That's what killed them both

Good morning to Goodnight- Eleni Kaur

We didn't have a perfect relationship
There's no such thing as a 'perfect
relationship'
We had our arguments but whatever
we had was lovely
I'll miss it forever but the memories
along with your scar,
permanently remain deep within my
heart.

Good morning to Goodnight- Eleni Kaur

26th November

Trying to look my best

Blue jumper

Black skirt

Straight hair

Favorite lip-gloss

You, on your lunch break

Now in front of me.

The way our eyes meet one
another's and we fall into
each other's arms

Your kisses on my

forehead

My desired ones

Good morning to Goodnight- Eleni Kaur

53 days ago

There was something about the
last time I saw you.

That's why I think everything
happens for a reason

It was as if I knew something was going
to happen-although I didn't.

I continuously told you 'I love you' and
I couldn't help saying it; it was every 2
minutes

The way we hugged and one
hand stroked my back- upwards
and downwards

Whilst the other, held my
hand-soft yet tight

O what a treasurable moment

There was something about when you
were about to leave too

I called your name

Good morning to Goodnight- Eleni Kaur

Tiptoed

Kissed your neck and told you I love you
once again-

I had never done that before; we
normally hugged and said goodbye

But this time

I called you back and kissed

you

and

that was it.

Good morning to Goodnight- Eleni Kaur

I craved your company.
I didn't want you to spend money on
me; I can provide for myself.
I wanted your time.
I desired your time and presence
I wanted to help you build this empire
so I can watch you succeed-
I wanted to be the girl who enthused
and kept you going.
I wanted to pick you up during
the difficult times
I wanted to watch you
succeed I wanted it to be me-
The woman behind it all- the woman you
turned to- the one who lent you an arm
when you needed a hand and stuck by
you through your highest of highs and
lowest of lows.
I wanted it to be me

I know how incredibly difficult it is to love someone with every inch of your body and soul and for it to end just like that, I know the pain. It aches not just the heart but the entire body. It's as if the entire skeleton becomes corrupted by sadness and the heart that pumps blood around your body is drained. It's so drained that it exhausts you; it no longer pumps the blood as fast as it used to; predominantly because your heart no longer beats as fast as it used to. Everything is worn out. Every inch of your body is tired. You loved wholeheartedly, with not just your heart but your mind, spirit and soul. You gave them the love you wanted back because you saw their potential- in fact, you still see their potential and it has corrupted you. You have had such a big fall down and you've never felt so low-they didn't intentionally mean to leave you feeling worthless; they claimed they want you to be happy.

But, 'how can I be happy?' you ask yourself
You've fallen so deep that now you're the only person who has to hold your own hand and help yourself up
But
You will
You will find yourself again
'Patience is a virtue.'

Good morning to Goodnight- Eleni Kaur

Goodnight

The day has ended
(indicative of closure)
The stars appear- wishing
becomes apparent.
No matter how much you try and
convince yourself during the day you
no longer miss the individual- it will kick
in during the night.
You make your way to a coffee shop-a
busy 2pm- the one just down the road
from school or work- telling yourself 'no
I don't miss them'
Hit 2am. That's when it'll hurt.
When you're laying in an empty
room reminiscing the memories-
The way you appreciated
this individual's existence
The amount of love you had for
them The spark you both created
when getting to know one another
Now,
Staring at the blank ceiling
Wondering either- why did they let me
go? Or- why did I let them go?
That's when it'll hit that nobody in the
world will ever love you the same

Good morning to Goodnight- Eleni Kaur

way;
Their love
cannot be
reciprocated.
Ever.
Enclosed still
Tears?
Maybe.
you turn to your side and think of all
the memories or what you could have
been.
The tears hit the pillows
You see a stain of warm
water Almost puddle-like
At this point, you're either wondering
what's wrong with me? Why did
they leave?
Or
Why did I let them go?
Maybe I wasn't ready?
Making up scenarios excuses
over-thinking
Blaming yourself for either doing
something wrong maybe not
treating them with enough love-
Or, still laying, staring at the blank
ceiling recalling the 'good morning' to
'goodnight' texts

Good morning to Goodnight- Eleni Kaur

Just to ponder upon the fact-No
matter how much you adored
them
No matter how many memories
you both created,

The spark has now been
lit out.

it's time for closure

Maybe one day you'll be his and he'll be yours

Maybe you'll find one another
Maybe he'll come home-

If not in this world

Maybe, just maybe in the next

Good morning to Goodnight- Eleni Kaur

Knowing the small things he didn't like
but still had to experience, killed her

She wanted to be the one who would
pick him back up

Gently lay her hand upon his cheeks
and tell him she would be there for
him and support him no matter what
life threw at him

Wrap her arms around him when he had
a rough day

She just wanted to be there for
him-Through both

His ups
and his

downs

Good morning to Goodnight- Eleni Kaur

She craves your presence
she craves your warm breath to be
reflected on her skin -the same
skin you left such a mark on that it
yearns to feel your touch
she craves her fingers running
through your soft hair with her
eyes looking deep into yours Open
your eyes;
She craves nothing but you

oNly YoU

Good morning to Goodnight- Eleni Kaur

I am always writing for him

The person who imprinted himself so deep into

my soul

That when I pick up a pen

All I want to do is cover the page with his name

Good morning to Goodnight- Eleni Kaur

So it's nearly the New Year
I stare expressionlessly at
my phone
Your name printed on the top left
corner
Asking myself 'should I message?'
Constantly repeating 'Not even a Happy
New Year x'
?
Then I realize.
If you want me, you'll fight.
My love for you is strong- you
said yourself you 'feel it'
So
If you want me
you'll come find
me

Good morning to Goodnight- Eleni Kaur

When I know I want something

I'll go for it

I'll fight for it

I won't give up

Neither should you

Because

If someone is always on your mind-They're most likely supposed to be there.

Good morning to Goodnight

Waking up to a good morning message
made my day
You were my good morning to
goodnight.
Now I'm sat here wondering why good
morning is two words and goodnight
is one
Maybe because in the morning you part
ways and you have the opportunity to
create your own story each day.
In the night, that's when the deep
conversations take place - we
come together to tell each other
our daily stories
That's when you get a real insight into
an individual.
The best time to talk
I remember
You and I
Conversations lasting until 3-
4am during the summer nights
Truth or dare
Dare I say
I object and create my own
Worse they were.
'Tell me a story'

3 full months you waited

Good morning to Goodnight- Eleni Kaur

Finally.

A uniquely composed one
Printed
Bound
Now- sat in a drawer- the one attached
to the bottom of my cupboard- the one
which very rarely gets opened.
Just to demonstrate I'm not the same as
the rest
Plus the pressure of hearing 'when
someone tells me a story it tells me a lot
about the person'
I wanted to spend time on it
Although you never got to physically
touch it, you still asked me to read it
aloud
I hope you felt it
I hope you felt how much you meant to
me

The Boy of Our Dreams

Conceived.
Cupped growing
Safe and sound
My precious, our precious
I had an idea of what he'd be
like My blood your blood
Mixed
Our first- excitement struck

I knew he was safe- safe inside
A place nobody could hurt him
warm cuddled
protected
Foetus now.
Gradually growing making me question
how very quick it was all happening

Kicking became apparent
I knew he had your crazy personality;
exemplified by the annoyingness of the
kicking and constant moving around Yet
appreciating these moments.
How you lay your gentle hands on
my belly
Just to feel your son's movements

Good morning to Goodnight- Eleni Kaur

tears of joy
melted heart

1am July 28th
Awoken by intense contractions
You yet not forgetting to give me
my good morning kiss
Continued contractions
Rushed to the hospital.

Room so delicately
luxuriously decorated
Simple yet so gorgeously designed
Glass Babies cot by my right
Blue blankie accompanied by a teddy
towards the far back
You, still by my side

Squeezing hands
Painful screams
Cries
And there he was- Our mini Singh!

Now wearing your first baby grow-

On my chest
Your right arm around me
Your left, slowly stroking our
son's delicate soft left cheek.

Good morning to Goodnight- Eleni Kaur

I took a deep gaze into your eyes
seeing how proud you were I
witnessed your tears of joy.
Your hand now entwined with mine
just like the first time we
encountered one another
Complimented with a kiss on the
forehead

Paternal grandparents
prouder than ever
Their first grandchild with their
only son- a mini you, he sure was.

Your eyes
My smile
Your hair
curly.
Gifted by his grandparents a
Silver stainless steel bangle
Accompanying his right wrist-
placed gently by his grandfather.

4pm- room filled with flowers
bluer than ever filled with
delight a part of you and part of
me He was here

3 Years of age.
Impeccable manners.

Good morning to Goodnight- Eleni Kaur

Courtesy to treat others with respect-
closeness with such a strong bond
between him and his grandfather.
Three generations all under one
roof-
Love, happiness a close-knit
family All we ever wanted.

Not only responsible for being a
husband and wife but now being a
mother and father of a beautiful little
boy A mini you
(a part of you a part of me!)
Our little boy- the one you had always
wanted.
This impeccable little
human Created by us

'You're going to be the mother of my
kids' he said.
That's when my imagination went into
deeply desired wonders

Good morning to Goodnight- Eleni Kaur

The purple pillow of yours which was my
favorite

(The one matching my preferred purple
top- remember the one I used to wear all
the time during our summer nights?)

The one I watched you fall asleep
and wake up on

Eternal love

I can still feel his wet lips
pressing sweetly against mine
Butterflies intensified I still feel it

The taste,
O I remember
How could I possibly forget?
My first whom I was hoping would be
my last
I still see it
Him and me
Me and him
Him and I
I and him
Us
Together
Although our souls may not be together
Our bodies may not be together
We may not be together
My love is forever
eternal 'Love never dies'
he said Hopefully
I thought

The way your thumb did that
moving thing whilst holding my hand

The way I rested my head on
your shoulder

The way you used to move your hands
up and down my back when we hugged

The way we entwined hands and I
took a picture every time

The   way   these
extraordinary moments will
forever remain memories

Good morning to Goodnight- Eleni Kaur

The door was open but only a little.
I wasn't fully inside; it was partially
open- I wanted him to open it when
he was prepared
I didn't force it open; I didn't want
to So,
I kept my hand on the handle.
Sometimes, when I knew something
was going on over the other side,
my grip on the handle tightened Yet
with a
softer fragile touch.
I wanted him to know there
was someone at the other end
There.
A strong desire to come inside
Wanting to be the girl who
Came home. To ignite the fire within him
Motivate him
;
I saw the potential. His potential.
When he was ready
He could let me in
I could enter- I told myself.
Clueless of the thoughts going on over
the other side of the door,
shook the hand whose strong grip yet
partially remained
Chaotic thoughts

Good morning to Goodnight- Eleni Kaur

Nervous. Wanting to go inside
Little I knew what was going on.
The touch on the handle remained
Soft
Tense.
Softer
Tenser.
Until
Bang!
Shut
just like that.

Good morning to Goodnight- Eleni Kaur

I may not know how you're
feeling, she said.
But
I know when you're hurting-

she thought.

As much as you try to deny it, I know.

Honestly, babe, nothing's wrong he said
so reassuringly

But she knew.

She could hear it in his

voice.

She felt it

She wanted to help

She wanted him to know
She was here as much as he was for
her

Remember the time I asked you to look out of the window and stare at the moon- I found it astonishing that we were both looking at the same thing yet from different locations. Now, I look out the window- not only to make a wish upon a star but I wonder if you're doing the same too

Imperfection is perfection. Think of it this way. A crystal- with lots of imperfect pieces attached and formed to make one beautiful crystal. That's the way you should view your flaws and insecurities; they all combine to make this one significant individual.

You.

I hope I've left my mark as the girl who will love you like no other. I hope you remember me. The 'crazy' and 'weird' one; our story was different we were different- we were the complete opposite but got along so well

I loved you and you loved me

Good morning to Goodnight- Eleni Kaur

Candles lit
Lamps on
Fire
ignited
4 snug on their living room sofa.

Vanilla scent
dissipated Fuzzy boots
Hot coco
Hands entwined-just like the first time
A kiss on the forehead just like
morning time.

Little girl and little boy snug and warm
between mother and father tightly
cuddled.
Curtains left undone
Snowflakes seen settling the ground

A loving family under one roof
Protection and love all around
That's all they wanted them to surround

A knock at the door the father goes
His friends and their wives appear
They were the family everyone loved
They were the ones everyone admired.

An hour or two, dinner set
Warmer and cozier than they'll ever
get the love within this home was

Good morning to Goodnight- Eleni Kaur

Contagious, Irresistible
Family, friends, neighbors all welcome

This home, in particular, was one
people felt at ease
For it contained the couple who loved
one another more than ever.
The ones who comforted and
advised The ones everyone looked
up to and aspired to be like

A place not only with a tightly knit
family around
But a home with lots of love to surround
A husband and wife with their two
children
The ones who inspired and believed in
others.

10pm now past children's bedtime
For it was a Friday night they deserved
family movie time
Guests thank these two for the
unexpected dinner
What a comfortable place it was
for people to be
They said they shall be back
sooner than ever!

Man and wife now prepare
children's milk and snacks

Good morning to Goodnight- Eleni Kaur

For this fortnightly Friday movie
night They eagerly awaited

Candles lit
Lamps on
Fire
ignited
4 snug on their living room sofa.

Sometimes the phone will light up
Sometimes the doorbell will ring
And all she hopes for is
Nothing but him
On the other side

Good morning to Goodnight- Eleni Kaur

'I just want you to be happy' I just
want You to be happy too.

As much as it will ache to see you with
another, I hope she makes you happy. I
hope she gives you the world. I hope
she gives you the love you deserve. I
will envy her but if she makes you
happy then I'll be content.

Sometimes I'll be walking and I'll think of something funny and I'll not help but think 'I need to tell him this.' I used to tell you the smallest to the biggest occurrences during my daily life but now when something happens I can't help but think 'I need to tell him this'- just to realize There's nobody to ask how my day was and that we don't talk anymore

If I even achieved one thing out of all of this
by building the connection between himself
and God, not only through my prayers for
him but by convincing him to pray and
telling him to make visits to the Gurdwara
often, then I'm pleased

'You're in my kismat. I know it.'
 he said

Good morning to Goodnight- Eleni Kaur

I know it can be difficult especially
when you get into the habit of talking to
someone every night and suddenly,
they're not there-whether this be a
friend or a lover

Especially when they've engraved
such a mark that they'll forever remain
deep within your heart

I know the pain; I've felt it too

It all comes down to the one individual

The one you look for in everyone The

one you'll love like no other Him

Faith

One thing I do remember is asking you, back when we were just getting to know one another is when you last visited the Gurdwara
To which you replied 'I don't
even remember'

I don't know if I helped encourage you but seeing you go more often as we spoke, really warmed my heart. I don't know if I helped motivate you to go but I knew I was constantly on your back. I really hope you still visit regularly.

I know I am no longer a significant part of your life- I, therefore, have no right to tell you what to do anymore, but please go.

He will help you. He is one person who will listen when nobody else does. He will guide you.

I promise

Good morning to Goodnight- Eleni Kaur

She had nothing but good intentions

She wanted to look after you

She desired to build you-both spiritually
and mentally

She may have been a handful at times
but

Remember

She's different from everyone else you
know

She had the spark

She was ambitious

You know you knew it yourself

Nothing but good intentions and a pure
heart to love you with

Never forget

Mazelike world

Mazelike
puzzled
Not knowing which path to take
Having to
Stop.
Allowing the rain to drop. Warm water
Other times- the sun was brighter than
ever
Still
Confused
In the mazelike world.
You take your walk
Within the mystified world
Trying to find a way out
Trying to find the liberty you deserve
Walking through the maze
Time alone
Noticing small pieces on the ground
Those never noticed before
Constructing these pieces together
Joining.
Binding.
Continue walking
Until the end.

Good morning to Goodnight- Eleni Kaur

You're out the maze.
You've reached the end
Sun brighter than ever
And you've
Found Yourself

Good morning to Goodnight- Eleni Kaur

Missing someone is one of the most
awful feelings you can ever
experience. You'll be walking around
thinking of something funny to tell them
and it suddenly hits that you no longer
talk. You can wish on a number of
stars, throw as many coins in wishing
wells and make as many 11:11 wishes
but at the end of the day, if you've tried
your best, deep down you know there's
nothing more you can do
And
that's what aches the heart the most

Blink of an eye

From the sleepiness nights due to
laughter and one another's company
in August
to sleepiness nights of tears
and solitude in December

Good morning to Goodnight- Eleni Kaur

I still remember the very first time I
held your hand to the last

It was in a flash

Our light was let out ever so rapidly

The light I truly believed would last
a lifetime.

When someone believes such a thing

And for the candles to then burn out-

Aches the heart like no other
feeling in the world

Saturdays

Waking up on a Saturday morning
first thought: how you're on your way
to work.
How you're usually commuting
around 8 and how work starts at 9
How you take the latest break between
12 and 1
And how you finish at 3 and get out
by 3.20
I am utterly obsessed with
you And it's so wrong
Because I wasn't even fought for.

Sundays

We used to spend most of our
Sundays together-

Facetiming or over the

phone So much joy

And now- a Sunday afternoon

A tight throat

Warm tears

Nearly 2 months of not speaking

I'm sat here writing this

You get so fed up that you feel empty
You're pissed off- out of love- most
likely.
There's a part of you that'll still care
It'll always care
The care is
Eternal Everlasting.
The reason why you're fed up is
because you put in your all
You wanted only the best for this
certain individual
It's as if it was all taken too seriously.
There are many people who are just 'not
ready.'
Sometimes people just enter lives at the
wrong time.
You're both young. Very young. Maybe
just maybe you constantly think

One day

Good morning to Goodnight- Eleni Kaur

From the smallest of things
The way your eyes looked into
mine before we kissed
The way you used to tease me
The way I'd ask for 10 kisses and
I'd be lucky enough to get 20
The way you held my hands and
your fingers intertwined with mine
The way the thought of you still
randomly makes a smile appear The
way you used to drink milk when you
were feeling too warm
The way you used to snore whilst
falling asleep
The memories
Our-memories
Will forever remain
Between
You and I
Only.
Every little piece of you
 I
Fell
For. I
Fell
Hard.
So hard; now that you're Gone- it
essentially pains and aches my
heart

Trapped between wanting to feel his physical touch which made everything seem alright or feeling his emotional touch which warmed the heart and soul

Good morning to Goodnight- Eleni Kaur

Trying to find yourself again after
making someone your priority,
putting them first-I loved it

I loved loving someone
It felt good
Knowing there was someone to
take care of him
Knowing there was someone who
would go out of their way to do anything
for him
It warned my heart
That person was
Me.
I'm not here to say nobody else will
do the same but I am certain nobody
will love him the way I did
I know nobody will care for him the way
I did
I get asked almost every day
'Why do you still care?'
I care because I feel affection
for him more than anything
If I ever happen to cross his mind
It won't be the same
Of course, it won't

She was let go of so easily That's
what hurt the most But- this wasn't
an act of want from
either of them, rather something
they had to do.
It doesn't mean she shouldn't
still worry;
Yes she worries about his health
Yes she worries about him
coming home late
Yes she worries about him leaving
work on a chilly winter's evening, 5pm
when it's dark outside
Why?
Because he imprinted such an affectionate
mark on her that no matter how hard she
tries to forget, she cannot.

Good morning to Goodnight- Eleni Kaur

Speaking of the memories and not
knowing how their day was or if
their weekly routine has changed
is honestly so confusing
Not knowing how they
feel anymore
Every time you try to
stop thinking you can't;
it's impossible
Your mind will drift from certain
situations to him
You've tried to convince yourself
that he doesn't care so you
shouldn't
But that's impossible
How could you
possibly stop caring?

She

Yes
She will worry if you're home late
She'll be concerned if you're out
after midnight
She'll make sure you text her letting
you know you're safe
She'll make sure you're taking care
of your health
She'll be aware you don't get
influenced by the wrong
people She'll keep you on
track She'll keep you motivated
She'll make sure you're warm before
going out on a winter's day
She'll make sure you've eaten
She'll make sure you don't get
involved in anything silly
You keep telling yourself that;
As much as I hope and pray you find
someone who does fall in love with you
in this respect- you keep convincing
yourself that there will be another like
me

I am different.

Good morning to Goodnight- Eleni Kaur

She'll never be me.

Good morning to Goodnight- Eleni Kaur

She won't have her heart

You won't feel the same love

You never feel the same love twice.

You'll crave the love she offered

you

As much as you try,

You won't forget her.

She was different to the rest

She was one of a kind.

And she knew it

She prayed you'd find someone who
would love you like she did

(Boy, if she could place her heart
into somebody else's chest she
would)

But deep down even you knew nobody
else ever could ever replace her

A broken heart

I think once the heart is broken, nothing will be the same again. Yes, one can heal but it's never the same. You do become stronger- in fact, you become a lot stronger. You learn to find yourself and who you are. You grow up, you mature and you become bolder. It's all a learning process. Yes, it is all an experience. But, you'll never be the person you were before. As much as you try, it'll never be the same

I surprised myself really; I never thought I would have reacted in the way I did and to be fairly honest, I disappointed myself. I know I can live without a man- I like to believe that I am not only completely focused on my future but I am also highly determined. I guess it was the memories that I would miss- getting to know him, what he desired etc. I just wanted to be the woman who would motivate him and be along his side to help him achieve his dreams and goals.

Good morning to Goodnight- Eleni Kaur

She still envisages everything you could
have been. The things you could have
done. Maybe this whole thing happened
because one day the both of you will
come back stronger than ever. (She
doesn't know. And neither does he.)
One day, it will all make sense. You're
oblivious to it now

but

one day- the both of you will know.

Good morning to Goodnight- Eleni Kaur

Am I pissed off? Yes. I am so mad at
you- To be honest, I'm hurt more than
anything because my only intentions
were to keep you happy and shower
you with my love. We wanted to be each
other's futures
I hate you but love you at the same
time. My love will always outweigh my
anger towards you; when I'm angry
with you, it is out of love.

Sometimes no matter how hard you try
No matter how much effort you put in,
Some things are just not meant to be.
In the moment, it really makes you
question whether happy endings really
do exist.
But it's important to remember that
eventually, everything will fall into
place Everything will be okay As they
say
'In the end, it'll all be okay
If it's not okay, it's not the end'

Good morning to Goodnight- Eleni Kaur

Laying on your back

Ears covered

Flicking through your phone

Literally touching the screen where
their picture is perfectly printed

Hoping to feel their touch.

Volume loud

Blank ceiling

The thought of someone else's touch

Tightened throat

Tightened chest

Tense

Thoughts of opening up to
someone else

Eyes closed
You try to sleep.

Lost appetite

I think it's very simple to lose
yourself when a situation akin to
heartbreak occurs
There will be days you can't eat
you lose all appetite Apparent
insomnia
As time progresses you pick
yourself back up
You pick up the small pieces You
hold your own hand- literally.
Look in the mirror and tell yourself 'I
can do this'
This normally happens late.

Night.

Memories of when you used to speak
start to kick in
You constantly wonder what you could
have done to have kept what you had

Memories you don't ever want to forget

Good morning to Goodnight- Eleni Kaur

I wonder if you still think of me If I ever
cross your mind Once in a blue moon
maybe? Whether at work, walking
down a street, seeing something, even
something small that makes me appear
in your mind

In a way, I hope it doesn't have the
same impact on you as it does on me
But,
The selfish me wants your throat to
tighten,
Your heart to skip a beat.
And I want you to miss
me. Yes,
I want you to miss me.
O how goddamn selfish of me
I want you to remember my voice
I want you to remember the way I
loved you
I want you to recollect our late night
conversations
I want it to all come rushing
in I want your mind full of
nothing but me
O how selfish
I hope you still have my scarf. It was
one I wore often. I wonder if my
scent has remained.

Good morning to Goodnight- Eleni Kaur

I wonder if you can still smell me
Only you know

Good morning to Goodnight- Eleni Kaur

There's almost a sense of
hesitancy Becoming close to
anyone else. Whether it be a friend
or a potential lover-
It sucks.
Yet, in a way it prepares
and teaches you how to
enjoy personal company;
You spend more time with yourself
An opportunity to boost your confidence
With more time to love yourself.
All because one person left -
constantly forcing you to wonder what
you did so wrong when you put in your
all to keep them happy-loved them
more than anyone
you're terrified to become close to
another-
A reminder that you're one person
that'll stay for eternal life
So,
Fall in love with yourself
Since you're the one person who
won't leave

5th October

On the phone

What a relief

Yet panic still kicks in

'Let me fix my hair'

Still on the phone

Walking faster Pace

increases Heart

starts pounding

Excitement kicks

Finally.

I see you. In a corner

We hug I look into your eyes and
fall into your arms once again

Tiptoeing arms around your neck

Good morning to Goodnight- Eleni Kaur

Head buried between your
shoulder and neck

What an amazing moment. (To be
in the arms of the first boy I fell in
love with!)

We start to walk

Hands tangled I

grab yours

Kiss them.

You take mine

Start to rub

them.

'Relax' you say

'Why are you so nervous?' Not knowing
how to respond- I hug you again

Continuously

Walking.

Stopping.

Good morning to Goodnight- Eleni Kaur

Falling into your arms.

We cross the road.

You wrap your arms around my
neck from behind

I take your hands

Kiss them once again

You move to my right

I clench your hand, tight.

Going into someone's back garden

Where it clearly says 'strangers will
be persecuted'

Looking deep into one another's
eyes with such happiness

Dreamlike.

You cup my face into your hands

I fall into your arms once more

Head buried between your neck and
shoulder

Good morning to Goodnight- Eleni Kaur

On my tiptoes-
I hug you tighter

We start to walk again

You say my name.
I love the way it rolls of your tongue

Finally.

We walk into the park- side by side

'Describe the scenery' you say

'the grass was as green as...as green
as' unable to finish my sentence

I take another look at you
without hesitation and kiss you.

'is that the lake?' I ask nervously

You laugh and mock me. Of course, it
was the lake. Silly me.

We find a place to sit. Facing the
lake leaves on the ground

Good morning to Goodnight- Eleni Kaur

You put me on your lap My

arms around your neck

I can't happen but rest my head on
your shoulder

'Isn't it crazy how you were just an
ordinary boy a couple of months ago?'
I say

'I still am that boy.'

'Not to me'

'What am I then?'

I raise my head

Looking deep into one another's eyes

I go one way

You go the

other.

lips now entwined

butterflies aroused

my heart beating fast

Good morning to Goodnight- Eleni Kaur

We take a moment

My First Kiss!

We continue

'I love you' I say

'I love you too' I hear. It was the
first time you said it!

Just you and I. Alone. A time to cherish.
Us, in each other's presence. I loved it.

I lay my head into your shoulder
once again

Shivering- you take off your red
checked shirt and put it around me

A gesture that demonstrated
your personality perfectly.

An hour and a half later we get up
and walk again

Around the block

Good morning to Goodnight- Eleni Kaur

You take my bag and hold it for me.

There were moments when you
attempted to wrap my scarf around me-
I taught you the way I wear it. My
maroon one, remember?

I wonder if you still know how
I shawl it around me

We continue to walk

We stop.

I look at you

Tiptoe

We kiss.

We continue walking

6.45pm dark.

October. Hands still

entwined Nearly 7pm.

I don't want to let you go at this point

Reluctant to say goodbye

Good morning to Goodnight- Eleni Kaur

'We have to do this again' you

say 'Yes, we do'

October 5th, 2016

Not only the day of my first

kiss But

One of the best days of my life

Good morning to Goodnight- Eleni Kaur

She knew when something was wrong-

She felt it deep within her heart

No matter how much he denied it

She knew.

And it killed her. As it would
kill anyone.

Knowing the one you love is going
through something and you're unable
to help, destroys you-

She tried to let herself in

But couldn't.

It killed her; do boys talk to one another
when something is hurting?

She knew things but had no way to
help- her thoughts were always with
him even though they were no longer
each other's responsibility

;

Good morning to Goodnight- Eleni Kaur

He let her go

The idea of someone else's arms wrapped
around his neck
Made her swallow
Hard.
The fact that she won't care if she's
hugging with not only her body but her
entire soul
Hurt.
The fact that she won't love
as wholeheartedly
Hurt.
The fact that she won't
understand things the way I did
Hurt.
Every little thing she will do - She
won't take her time to make sure it's
performed to the best of her ability.
Will she write you love letters?
Will she make you dispose of the letters
I stayed up writing?
Who knows?
But the idea of her not loving as
deeply as me
Hurt more than anything.

From the time when I was on your
back to shaving your beard and when
you finally did I told you I missed it and
I didn't even receive a good morning
text the following morning
To our silly arguments when you'd
call me names and I'd ask for 10
kisses in order to accept your apology

I miss it all

Good morning to Goodnight- Eleni Kaur

It's insane thinking in a few months you
could thoroughly be forgotten

I by no means want to
ask 'remember me?'

Nobody wants to be forgotten

Especially someone who loved with
every inch of their soul-

I hope I've left such a significant
mark that you'll never forget

'Love you x' reads the last message
you sent

15.12.16

Good morning to Goodnight- Eleni Kaur

The thought of falling in love again
terrified her
How could she even think of
moving on when her heart told
her it was so incredibly wrong to
seek affection, salvation and love
from any other spirit than yours

Good morning to Goodnight- Eleni Kaur

Two hearts full of nothing but perpetual love

Good morning to Goodnight- Eleni Kaur

The way his eyes lit up when he saw you
The way his smile gave you such warmth
How his smile warmed you in ways nothing else
ever could
His joy was your delight
All you wanted was to see him happy
His essence
His integrity
His touch
Everything about him excited you

Unquestionably, someone that'll forever
remain deep within your heart Someone
who you will incessantly look
for in everyone you meet
Either because they were your first, or because
they gave you love like no other that they've
ended up imprinting their scar so far into your
soul that you'll look for them within everyone
you encounter

Good morning to Goodnight- Eleni Kaur

We simply went from strangers to building a strong friendship with getting into a relationship and becoming strangers again.

It's crazy because you're the one person I opened up to. The one person who I felt comfortable talking to. The one individual to whom I ranted many problems to without hesitation. The one individual who was always here for me whenever I was at my happiest as well as darkest of times. The person who I'd go to for advice- the person whose number I'd have printed on my phone screen whenever I felt unsafe- knowing you were just a phone call away

And for that, I am forever grateful.

'We're going to make this work'

He told her

Good morning to Goodnight- Eleni Kaur

Our love was only summer

lasting I had to remind myself

'There is no flower brighter than the
first to bloom after a harsh winter.'

Good morning to Goodnight- Eleni Kaur

She had nothing but a pure heart to
love with
She kept to herself and focused on
her own work
Her priorities were straight in the
sense that independent success was
always on her mind
She prioritized her work and kept to
herself
When she loved, she loved hard
Maybe she was too much because
she loved 'too much'

Good morning to Goodnight- Eleni Kaur

I wonder if you still read the letters I
wrote you-
The ones I stayed up until 4am- articulating,
drafting, rewriting, perfecting
Spending time shamelessly selecting the
prettiest paper and handpicking the cutest
envelope to enclose my words within
Something I never told you

Good morning to Goodnight- Eleni Kaur

My four day trip to Italy before the attachment-

After touristic days out, I'd come back to the hotel room that I shared with my mother

Whilst she was fast asleep I'd jump out of bed and go into the corner where I'd lay my cushions and feel so snug

I would sit upon a wooden desk- back laid upon the wall with a pillow resting behind me- phone plugged in the socket charging

Comfier than ever

And

I'd talk to you.

I was only an hour ahead of our standard time

but in spite of being exhausted after an adventurous day, I'd stay awake just to talk to you.

Good morning to Goodnight- Eleni Kaur

Bearing in mind this was just the first week of us getting to know one another- I had never felt so warm- I felt at ease- I enjoyed each minute of last summer- I was blissful; I would look forward to waking up to a message from you, I'd look forward to exploring Italy and I would look forward to coming back to the hotel to speak to you

I treasured every moment of it

Good morning to Goodnight- Eleni Kaur

She knew his form of escapism

She didn't want him to feel in solitude

She didn't want him to harm himself not
knowing the damage he was causing

She wanted to be his

comfort She even wished he

heard her calling out his

name She wanted to be His

one and only

Good morning to Goodnight- Eleni Kaur

I wonder how you've been feeling
each day

I know things that remain only
between you and me

I don't ever want you to go through
anything alone

I hope you find someone who cares
as much as I do

I hope you find someone who craves
your presence as much as I do

I hope you find someone who holds
your hand as tightly as I did

I hope you find someone who
cherishes you

Good morning to Goodnight- Eleni Kaur

When he left

He took every inch of her with him

Summer Love

I dread the approaching summer
The thought of you and me
during last summer
The memories we created will
be treasured for sure
Those nights we spent getting to
know each other
To slowly falling for one another It
hurts knowing you could be with
someone else
It hurts knowing there could be
someone to whom you could say
'you remind me of someone'
which will most likely make her
form a strong dislike towards me-
her wanting you but you
remembering nothing but our
memories

Good morning to Goodnight- Eleni Kaur

Summer will return
Different- definitely
No more calls
No more talk of our
aspirations, hopes and
desires
Our 5-hour calls
Hearing you breathe down the
phone As you snore away
My smile appears
TV still running in the background
Oh you silly boy
You sleep I talk
You, still unaware of what I used to say

No more us

Good morning to Goodnight- Eleni Kaur

We went from phone calls lasting
5 hours to never speaking again.

'But everything was going so well'
you constantly hear.'

That's right- it was

Who knows what happened...

The possibility of such a bright and
successful future all banished- literally in
a blink of an eye

Leaving them both broken

Good morning to Goodnight- Eleni Kaur

Witnessing each other's innocent sides- both
of them
Late nights
Asking questions
Deep conversations
Closeness
Such a deep connection build by them
both Learning one other's stories
Learning each other's qualms and aspirations
Letting one another in
Now,

Just strangers with each other's secrets

You lose all motivation to love again.
The thought of loving someone else
physically makes you sick. This was the
person you wanted- the one you thought
you'd stay loyal to and spend the rest of
your life with.
This was the one person you felt at
home with. The one person who not
only made you feel intense
butterflies but eased you with their
intense comfortability.
Being in their arms made you feel safe
and at home. You thought these are
the arms where 'I'll forever remain.' You
didn't want to feel anyone else's
embrace; you wanted them and only
them.
And you still crave their presence

Good morning to Goodnight- Eleni Kaur

The way we used to sleep over
the phone-

Hearing your every

breath

Warmed my heart

The nights when I

couldn't sleep and

you'd whisper and

wait for me to go to

bed

Those were the best

moments

The little things,

They meant the most

I've learned that sometimes people come into your life to show you who you can be and they can be someone to whom you literally spill your life to. Not everyone stays. But, we still have to be grateful for the things they've given us and wish them the very best

Good morning to Goodnight- Eleni Kaur

There will be nights where you'll find
yourself staring at the ceiling
reminiscing the memories you shared
with this certain individual. You'll desire
to re-live the moments. You'll yearn to
be in their arms- for their comfort- the
thought of their presence ignites the
warmth of your body with the warm
water flowing down your cheeks- but as
you wipe the tears away, you'll put your
hair up- either in a ponytail or a bun.
Tight. You'll look into the mirror and
you'll tell yourself that one day this will
all make sense. You have to convince
yourself that one day you're going to
wake up with the love of your life- you
might even be lucky enough to wake up
to a baby's cry and everything will be
satisfactory. You will be awoken by a
good morning kiss- you'll be with
someone who loves and cherishes you
to the extent of which no other human
being could.
You'll find out why it didn't work out with
anyone else. So, for now, my darling you
have to keep your head held high, focus
on your own happiness instead of

Good morning to Goodnight- Eleni Kaur

putting other people's before your own
as usual- focus on your own success
and keep working hard because

It will all make sense one day- I promise

Good morning to Goodnight- Eleni Kaur

As far as she's concerned,
he told her he was just as attached as
she was

It pained her no longer knowing

how he felt

Going from knowing his

everyday routine to knowing

nothing at all-

The unexpected phone calls

The calls after work

The way he grabbed her hand and
walked
the way he held her hands to
passionately kiss them

The way he kissed her

The way he bit her bottom lip
whilst fervently kissing her.

How she misses the sleepless
nights full of laughter

Constantly thinking of what happened to

whatever they had- was there anything she could have done differently? Was she not making him happy enough? Did she do something wrong? Was she too much?

So many questions- floating around her

mind

Unable to stop over thinking.

How very daunting to know how
quickly things have the capability
of changing

Maybe letting her go was a way of showing her how much you loved her; you did say you loved her- a lot of people tell her, 'maybe he didn't think he could make you as happy as someone else out there could' maybe that's the reason you let her go

Good morning to Goodnight- Eleni Kaur

He left such an imprint on your soul
that your body craves his essence

I think it's very important to remind ourselves that the heart is a complicated organ- it took 9 months to create and nothing and nobody should let it go through such intensity of pain in a matter of seconds

Good morning to Goodnight- Eleni Kaur

His laughter warmed me in ways
his shirt couldn't

It was hurtful more than anything, to
be honest
Giving so much love to someone
Someone who knew how much you
loved them

Just to join that pile of exs

Good morning to Goodnight- Eleni Kaur

I still pray for you

It's a habit- a habit that I don't want to take control over- something that happens naturally and I'm proud of

I remember the very first time I prayed for you- this will forever be an on-going act. I truly believe if you love a man, pray for him. It warms my heart when I ask The Almighty to look after you for me; I have full faith that he will. I pray for you whenever I pray for myself. I hope he guides you in the right direction towards the right path and I hope he never makes you feel alone;

If you love a man,

Pray for him

Good morning to Goodnight- Eleni Kaur

Nobody will have the same effect
upon you as he did.

His essence was something special

His touch gave you warmth both
internally and externally-

There was something special.

The way his eyes lit up when he smiled

The way he wrapped his arms around
your body

The way his thumb stroked your
hand when your hands were
entwined with one another's grip

The way his lips touched your forehead
with the kisses you loved the most

The way he licked his lips before
he leaned in to kiss you

Nobody else's mark will be
the same

Good morning to Goodnight- Eleni Kaur

You opened me up

You made me feel so comfortable that
I could talk to you about anything and
everything

'No one has loved me the way you have'

Good morning to Goodnight- Eleni Kaur

The attachment
The connection
Unordinary
Different- indeed
There was something
Something they had
They say opposites attract
But right now
It seems as though they're repelling

It still feels like a fresh wound
One that cannot (even by a
plaster) rectify
Forever waiting to be healed

The Boy in the Blue Suit

It all comes down to the boy in the blue suit. The boy I first laid my eyes on and couldn't get out of my mind. It was love at first sight- I still remember that feeling; it was something out of the ordinary.

Good morning to Goodnight- Eleni Kaur

There's always a constant thought
of what we could have been

Where we could have gone

All the plans we had

Where we'd live

The places we'd go

The smiles we'd share

The tears we'd shed

The children we'd bare

Good morning to Goodnight- Eleni Kaur

It was love of a mad girl they all said
We've never seen someone love
that much
She was one in a million
he himself said so

For the girl who comes after

There's a letter waiting to be opened
by you

But, just in case he doesn't give it Here's

a little something from me to you.

I don't know what else to say other than
simply starting with a hey.

It may be wrong of me to say but
nobody can love him this way

Love so strong it could kill

Love of a crazy girl they all said

Nevertheless, he's now yours

So please

Make sure when you hug him, you do it
right- not too tight but just alright

Hold his hand when he's down and
cheer him up when he has a frown

He has a sensitive side so make sure
to give him space

Good morning to Goodnight- Eleni Kaur

And make sure when you kiss him

You don't do it with such haste

He likes to take things slow

And he prefers things to gradually grow

Please be there to support him
in whatever decisions he makes

Look after his parents with such grace

There's something special about
him and the connection they have

So please be there for him.

Tell him to pray

Tell him to go to the Gurdwara

Build the connection between him and
God

Motivate him

Love him

And show him you care

Ask him how his day was

Good morning to Goodnight- Eleni Kaur

Make sure he's eaten

Make sure he's taking care of his health

Don't let him get involved in
anything silly or get involved with the
wrong people

Cherish every moment you have
with him and love every inch of him

Appreciate everything he does and
never take anything for granted

Because remember, there's
someone out here who would kill to
be in your place

Lots of love,

Me

Good morning to Goodnight- Eleni Kaur

'Nothing lasts forever' I said

'Love never dies' he said

With eternal love

The girl who loved you
more than the world

;

Essentially

You were my very first
good morning to
goodnight

I wrote this to reassure myself that this isn't a long break, rather something that's probably not written to be for this world. I wrote it because I need to reach a state of mind where I know I've done all that I can from my side. I hope I've demonstrated the idea of slowly picking yourself back up no matter how hard you may fall.

This book was for me to move forward along my journey; rather than constantly having those memories floating around my mind, I have them composed and safe in this book. But, it can also be considered as my final attempt before completely backing down. I wouldn't necessarily see it as 'giving up' rather, accepting that we're probably not meant to be.

I hope in at least 6 months' time I have reached peace with my mind; right now my thoughts are full of nothing but chaos and it's so important for me to find myself again.

Good morning to Goodnight- Eleni Kaur

If you have been through anything similar, I promise you everything takes it's time and whatever is meant to be in your life will come back. I cannot reiterate this enough- I know the thought of hearing that saying gives you some hope but at the same time, it tightens your throat- making you wonder 'what if we're not meant to be?' But, one day, it will all make sense.
Everything will make sense to

you. So, my darling-

Take all the time you need to heal.

Go out there

Explore life,

Live,

Love and appreciate every single breath you take;

Whatever is meant to be in your life,

No matter how far it may drift,

It will always come back- I promise.

Good morning to Goodnight- Eleni Kaur

Crafting this was almost a cathartic process- This book was inspired by an experience I encountered and I would hate for someone to go through what I did- I hated losing my appetite. I hated not having anybody to relate with (hence why I hope my words have shown you that you are not alone). I hated having to hear 'I looked up to you' or 'I admired you' but, it's those very words that pushed me to write this.

Although I may not be of any help in terms of helping you heal, I believe by printing the pain simply in black and white (literally!) almost reassures you that you are not alone in this world. At the same time I hope that I have convinced you to never give up on your dreams and what you love.

I guess moments like this have to occur in our everyday lives- it sucks but pain is necessary for change- it's vital for self-improvement. Also, heartbreak is inevitable- it's as if it needs to happen at least once in our lives. It sucks, Yes, it will be painful but you will find yourself. Although I'm not there yet, this book and my form of escapism (writing)   have really helped me along this journey. So, I urge you- yes, cry- let it all out- let out the pain; you need to! But, don't sit back and do nothing! If you want something, go out there and fight for it- never sit back and wait for things to fall into place.

A few words of advice:

Never ever say 'Maybe it just wasn't meant to be' if you didn't even try; if you don't try, you will never know!

I have recently fallen in love with self-help books and a quote I picked up from Rob Bell was '**how we respond to what happens to us- especially the painful, excruciating things that we never wanted and we have no control over- is a creative act.'**

This was my creative act. I went through a horrible situation but my 'creative act' was to write a book and hopefully inspire you to one day look at undesirable situations optimistically.

Nevertheless, I think when a situation like this occurs; all we can do is wish the significant other nothing but the very best for their future.

Good morning to Goodnight- Eleni Kaur

I would just like to reiterate to my readers- never give up on what you love. Always fight and keep on going; no matter how far you may fall down, you're the only one that's going to pick yourself back up. Fight for what you truly believe in. If you want something go out there and get it-

Fight; (this is mine!)

Take risks and never give up

For, 'the only thing worse than death is a regret filled coffin.'

Good morning to Goodnight- Eleni Kaur

<u>For the boy in the blue suit:</u>

I hope you're doing great. I understand this situation must have been difficult for you also. As you told me, you want me to be happy and I really want you to be happy too. I've stated this in many of the letters I gave you (which I hope you still have!) but I wish you tones of success and happiness for the future; you truly deserve it.

Thank you for the memories you gave me. Thank you for putting up with me (even though I was probably a handful at times.) Thank you for being my first kiss and for making that moment special. Thank you for making me feel loved. Thank you.

As I've mentioned before, maybe this was just a touch of fate; in life, you don't always get what you want. Yes, I am a firm believer of the saying 'everything happens for a reason' and I guess if we're meant to be, we'll drift back together- some way or another. If maybe one day you think that I'm the one for you, then one day we might decide to pursue this further; right now, we're both young and we have our whole lives ahead of us- so we might just find one another again. But, if we're not meant to be, we cannot force it- one thing I've definitely had to come to terms with!

This was painful to write but I enjoyed most moments; writing about the good times made me feel as if I was living them all over again.

Neither of us know what the future holds or what's in our destiny and that's both frightening yet exciting.
Once again, you will forever have this place deep inside my heart. But, for the woman who will come next, I hope and pray she gives you unconditional love, I pray she brings out the best in you- as much as I wanted to do this, maybe it just wasn't supposed to be done by me. Although I may no longer hold a significant part of your life, I'm going to be here, always. Don't ever feel hesitant to message me if you need someone to talk to- whether it be 3am or 5pm; after all,

Good morning to Goodnight- Eleni Kaur

I   was   a   girl   you   once   loved

Good morning to Goodnight- Eleni Kaur

For a chance to feature on @EleniiSophia's Instagram page, be sure to share your favorite poems via social media with the hashtags:

#GoodMorningToGoodnight #GMTGN #EleniSophia

Thank you- and remember, none of this will matter in a year's time so it's definitely not worth stressing over - focus on yourself, spend time alone to figure out what you really want and live life to its fullest!

Lots of love,

Eleni
X

Good Morning to
Goodnight was
originally self-
published in 2017.
However, it was then
republished in 2020
under Publishing
Firm, Perspective
Press Global.

Made in the USA
Coppell, TX
05 January 2022

70718401R00100